W9-BXY-292

Thunder on the Plains

For Misha, who chased the buffalo

For numerous instances of helpfulness, kindness, and/or accommodation, inter alia, the author would like to thank: Harvey Payne of the Nature Conservancy's Tallgrass Prairie Preserve in Pawhuska, Oklahoma; the owners of the Triple U Buffalo Ranch, near Pierre, North Dakota (locally called the Houck Ranch); Nina Cummings of the Photography Department at the Chicago's Field Museum; and Professor Carole Mandryk of Harvard University's Department of Anthropology.

Atheneum Books for Young Readers
An imprint of Simon & Schuster Children's Publishing Division
1230 Avenue of the Americas
New York, New York 10020
Text copyright © 2001 by Ken Robbins
All rights reserved, including the right of reproduction in whole or in part in any form.
Book design by Angela Carlino
The text of this book is set in Graham.
Printed in Hong Kong

Library of Congress Cataloging-in-Publication Data
Robbins, Ken.
Thunder on the plains : the story of the American buffalo / by Ken Robbins.
p. cm.
Summary: A brief introduction to the history of the American buffalo and how it was almost hunted into extinction.
ISBN 0-689-83025-4 (alk. paper)
1. American bison—History—Juvenile literature. [1. Bison. 2. Endangered species.]
I. Title.
QL737.U53 R58 2001
599.64'3'0978—dc21 00-021426

FIRST EDITION

KEN ROBBINS

Thunder
on the Plains

The Story of the American Buffalo

ATHENEUM BOOKS FOR YOUNG READERS

New York   London   Toronto   Sydney   Singapore

This is the story of a great shaggy creature, a very American beast, one found here and nowhere else. Perhaps you've seen one on an old nickel or heard about how so many of them once roamed the land. Among the legends of the American West, there were stories of vast and mighty herds two hundred miles long. These herds took two days, moving along at a pretty good pace, to pass a particular point. The sky would darken from the dust they raised, and when they took it in their minds to run, they made a sound like thunder on the plains.

In 1875 there were perhaps fifty million of them. Just twenty-five years later nearly every one of them was gone. No one had thought that, with so many around, they could ever nearly disappear, but in the end it didn't take very long.

AMERICAN BUFFALO

The Lakota Sioux people called this creature "Tatonka," a word which also means "spirit." Technically speaking, they are bison. Their closest relation is known as the wisent, a different species of bison that once, long ago, was common in western Europe. But the wisent had disappeared from there long before the first Europeans came here. So when the Europeans did arrive, and they saw the American bison, they may have had other creatures in mind. Perhaps they were reminded of pictures they had seen of Asian or African buffalo. In any case, "buffalo" is what they called the bison, and today either name is equally right.

WISENT

WATER BUFFALO

CAPE BUFFALO

ONE OF THE FIRST DRAWINGS OF A BUFFALO EVER MADE BY A EUROPEAN

BUFFALO CALF

Sixty million years ago gigantic dinosaurs lived in North America. Today nothing nearly so large walks the land. We do have moose and elk and deer and antelope and bears. There are mountain lions, mountain sheep, and mountain goats still here—all pretty big, (especially the moose) but none of them compares with the buffalo. Only six feet tall, but as heavy as a car, the American bison is by far the most massive wild animal in America today.

How did the buffalo get here? Fifty thousand years ago, there was a bridge of land connecting Asia and Alaska. It's now covered by the sea, but back then some of the ancient Asian ancestors of our modern buffalo wandered east across that bridge looking for food to eat. The buffalo of that day were even bigger than the buffalo we have today, and they were slightly different in other ways; one, called "Bison Latifrons," had very wide horns.

BISON LATIFRONS SKULL

MODERN BISON SKULL

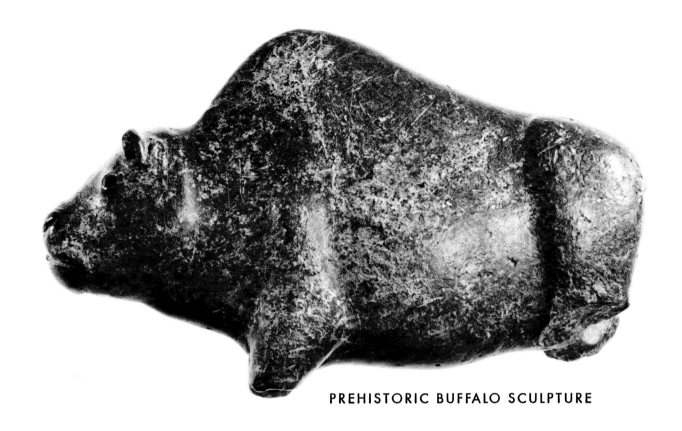

PREHISTORIC BUFFALO SCULPTURE

The first human beings to come to America were, as far as we know, not the Vikings, or even Columbus and his men. They were wandering hunters and their families—brave and hungry Asian souls. Some, no doubt, followed the buffalo and other animals across that land-bridge from Asia. The people we call Indians—all the tribes of North and South America—were descended from those men and women.

For men and buffalo, the journey across the land-bridge to Alaska was worth the effort, though it probably didn't seem that way at first. An ice age—a time of very bitter cold—had left the valleys of the northwest blocked with ice and snow. For a while it may have seemed that there was no escape from the harsh conditions there. In fact it may have taken centuries for them to find their way over mountains and across rivers, thousands of miles to the grassy plains that lay to the south in central North America. But there, with plenty of food and room to roam, the buffalo thrived and their numbers grew.

At that time, it's true, there were many more wolves than we have today. Along with other predators, they would certainly have preyed on the buffalo. But a buffalo, as you can imagine, is very strong; its kick can kill and its horns are long and deadly. A single wolf against a large, healthy bison wouldn't have a chance. Even a pack of wolves would rather attack the sick or weak, and leave the rest alone. In that way, the wolves just made it easier for the stronger ones to survive. And there were not so many humans, yet, to kill the buffalo.

As human beings spread out into every part of the land, some stayed in the north, some wandered south. All of them—wherever they were—had to live on whatever they could. Some learned to hunt and fish; some learned to grow their own foods; some learned to gather fruit, berries, and edible roots. But for those who lived on the great wide plains, the buffalo was everything.

From long experience on the plains, the Indians developed many ways of hunting, and one of them was called "the buffalo jump." A few braves would chase a buffalo herd to get them running, and other men on either side would wave their arms and try to guide the charging herd to the edge of a cliff. The buffalo in front would have no choice: when they got to the cliff they'd have to jump off; and of course, they'd be killed by the fall. At the bottom of the cliff other members of the tribe would wait to skin the hides and divide the meat. Everybody got a share.

BUFFALO BONES USED AS PAINT DAUBERS

BUFFALO DEW CLAWS TIED WITH
LEATHER THONGS TO MAKE A RATTLE

BUFFALO TAIL WHISK

Of course, the Indians wanted the meat for food, but they used every other part of the buffalo as well: From the skin they made shirts and skirts and trousers and shoes, purses, boats, blankets and bedding, tipis for shelter, and the tops of drums. They carefully saved the bones and used them for knives and scraping blades, war clubs, peace pipes, and musical whistles. They made necklaces of the teeth and used the stomachs like pots for cooking. The sinew made excellent thread for sewing; the horns made arrow points and bows; the hooves made glue. They used the skulls in religious rites, and even the dung was burned for fuel. It's not hard to imagine why they worshiped the spirit of the noble beast who gave them almost everything they needed.

For a very long time, it seems, the buffalo and the Indians shared the grasslands of North America well. The humans were not great in number, and they respected the buffalo, most often killing only as many animals as they needed. But foreigners from Europe arrived here with guns in 1492, and in the years that followed they kept coming—more and more. Some were bold explorers, looking for lands to claim in the name of their king; some were greedy men looking for gold; some were hunters and trappers; some were settlers. From these white men the native people got horses, and they, too, learned to hunt with guns. They had to share the land with these Europeans who often didn't treat them fairly, but the buffalo still roamed the plains, and several hundred years remained for the buffalo and the Indians before things really changed for the worse.

Over the next few centuries, more and more of these white people came, and wherever they went they wanted to own the land—something the Indians would never have thought to do. They wanted to dig the land for gold, and to farm the land for food, and they wanted the grassland so their livestock could feed. As these strangers took over more and more of the land, they and the Indians were often at war. In the middle of the nineteenth century they built a railroad across the plains, and wherever that railroad went, more people came, more houses were built, and more fields were plowed. The places where the buffalo once had roamed were being turned into farms and towns.

In the 1880s the buffalo herds were still beyond counting, but white hunters took a terrible toll. Hundreds of animals were slaughtered each day to feed the U. S. Army, and it is horrible to believe, but many buffalo were killed just so that the Indians would have nothing to eat. Some hunters killed them just for their tongues or their hides—a terrible waste. Some, for "fun," even rode on the railroad trains, and shot them from the windows, leaving them behind altogether to rot on the plains.

By 1910 the killing was over and we had created a national shame. Of the millions of buffalo that once roamed the plains, just five hundred or so were all that remained. (Not to mention the fact that Indian nations had been lied to and cheated, scattered, defeated, and forced to abandon their old ways of life.)

Slowly but surely people came to their sense when they realized just exactly what had been done. Laws were passed and preserves were established where buffalo herds could be cared for and be safe. At the last possible moment the buffalo was saved from extinction—two hundred thousand are living today. They are raised on ranches and they are used for food, because their meat tastes like beef, and it's healthier, too. There are even a few places where these magnificent creatures are allowed to roam about more or less free—a few hundred here, a few thousand there. The American buffalo is no longer endangered—we certainly ought to be happy about that. But there is one further thing that we should want to remember: the millions are gone, and they will never be back.

PHOTO CREDITS IN ORDER OF APPEARANCE

Buffalo herd (Tallgrass Prairie, Pawhuska, Oklahoma) photo by Ken Robbins

Solitary bull (Lawton, Oklahoma) photo by Ken Robbins

Buffalo head nickel photo by Ken Robbins

Wisent photograph by P. V. August, courtesy of the Mammal Slide Library, American Society of Mammalogists

Cape buffalo photo by Ross Warner, courtesy of the Warner Mammal Slide Library, American Society of Mammalogists

Water buffalo photo by P. V. August, courtesy of the Mammal Slide Library, American Society of Mammalogists

Primitive buffalo drawing by Francisco Lopez de Gomara from *La Historia General de las Indias* (second edition), 1554

Composite photo (moose and bison); Moose photo by Bryon Jorjorian, courtesy of Bryon Jorjorian Photography. Bison photo by Ken Robbins

Buffalo calf photo by Ken Robbins

Bison Latifrons skull, courtesy of the Department of Library Sciences, American Museum of Natural History

Bison effigy, courtesy of the Glenbow Museum (Calgary, Alberta, Canada)

Mountains and glacier (Olympia National Park, Washington) photo by Ken Robbins

Buffalo on the plains (Houck Ranch, near Pierre, North Dakota) photo by Ken Robbins

Wolves Attacking Buffalo painting by William De La Montaigne Cary, courtesy of the Glenbow Museum (Calgary, Alberta, Canada)

The Silk Robe (circa 1890) painting (oil on canvas) by Charles M. Russell, courtesy of the Amon Carter Museum (Fort Worth, Texas)

American Buffaloe after Titian Ramsay Peale, 1832, hand-colored lithograph, courtesy of the Amon Carter Museum (Forth Worth, Texas)

Buffalo Hunt (circa 1858) painting by Alfred Jacob Miller, courtesy of Western Canada Pictorial Index, Inc.

Driving buffalo off a cliff engraving by Theodore R. Davis, *Harper's Magazine,* January 1869

Buffalo bone paint daubers (H65.313.13-16) courtesy of the Provincial Museum of Alberta (Edmonton, Alberta, Canada)

Dew-claw rattle (H65.177.1) photo courtesy of the Provincial Museum of Alberta (Edmonton, Alberta, Canada)

Buffalo-tail expunger (H65.251.19) photo courtesy of the Provincial Museum of Alberta (Edmonton, Alberta, Canada)

Buffalo Hunting painting (1863) by George Catlin, courtesy of the Autry Museum of Western Heritage

The Honyocker photograph by L. A. Huffman, courtesy of the Montana Society (Helena, Montana)

Shooting buffalo on the line of the Kansas Pacific Railroad photo from *Frank Leslie's Illustrated Newspaper,* courtesy of the Kansas State Historical Society

Buffalo hunting in eastern Montana engraving. Artist unknown, courtesy of the Kansas State Historical Society

Buffalo hunt near Scott's Bluff, Nebraska, engraving. Artist unknown, courtesy of the Kansas State Historical Society

Pile of buffalo skulls photo. Photographer unknown, courtesy of the Burton Historical Collection, Detroit Public Library

Rath and Wright's Buffalo Hide Yard (Dodge City, Kansas) photo (circa 1874) by R. Douglas, courtesy of the Amon Carter Museum (Fort Worth, Texas)

Buffalo at Tallgrass Prairie (Pawhuska, Oklahoma) photo by Ken Robbins

Nursing buffalo calf (Tallgrass Prairie, Pawhuska, Oklahoma) photo by Ken Robbins